SUITOR

SUITOR

poems

Joshua Rivkin

Red Hen Press | *Pasadena, CA*

Book design by Mark E. Cull

Library of Congress Cataloging-in-Publication Data

Names: Rivkin, Joshua, author.
Title: Suitor : poems / Joshua Rivkin.
Description: First edition. | Pasadena, CA : Red Hen Press, [2020]
Identifiers: LCCN 2020002078 (print) | LCCN 2020002079 (ebook) | ISBN
  9781597098588 (trade paperback) | ISBN 9781597098199 (ebook)
Subjects: LCGFT: Poetry.
Classification: LCC PS3618.I894 S85 2020 (print) | LCC PS3618.I894
  (ebook) | DDC 811/.6—dc23
LC record available at https://lccn.loc.gov/2020002078
LC ebook record available at https://lccn.loc.gov/2020002079

The National Endowment for the Arts, the Los Angeles County Arts Commission, the
Ahmanson Foundation, the Dwight Stuart Youth Fund, the Max Factor Family Foun-
dation, the Pasadena Tournament of Roses Foundation, the Pasadena Arts & Culture
Commission and the City of Pasadena Cultural Affairs Division, the City of Los Angeles
Department of Cultural Affairs, the Audrey & Sydney Irmas Charitable Foundation, the
Kinder Morgan Foundation, the Meta & George Rosenberg Foundation, the Albert and
Elaine Borchard Foundation, the Adams Family Foundation, the Riordan Foundation,
Amazon Literary Partnership, and the Mara W. Breech Foundation partially support Red
Hen Press.

First Edition
Published by Red Hen Press
www.redhen.org

for my parents

CONTENTS

He does not keep it fine
by innocence or leaving things out.

—Jack Gilbert
"Prospero Without His Magic"

And everything is forgiven, and it would be strange not to forgive.

—Anton Chekhov
Notebook of Anton Chekhov

ONE

The Suitors

My mother's third boyfriend owned a Peugeot
he let me drive over the Choptank River Bridge.
He wore cedar aftershave, a camel hair coat.
He opened his framing shop for business
almost every Tuesday and Wednesday afternoon.

He told me adult jokes, bought me a racing kite,
took me out with golf buddies
who drank G&Ts and would bet on anything—
chip shots, baseball games, the cup size
of the waitresses at the Hole-in-One.

Once, for a costume party, he dressed as a pimp.
Gold chains, leather coat, a peacock
feather tucked in the hat's band.
He came over in blackface.
My mother wore fishnets,
a tight red dress, matching lipstick,
blue-cloud eye shadow.

His shoe-polish skin, her fever dress,
our family on the front lawn—
there is no way to catalog or camouflage
this moment. I've tried. It's like a kite
caught in a tree high above ground,
and there's no way to bring it down
without breaking it, or the branches.

His DREAMHOUSE between ambition and collapse—
blueprints for a shaky foundation, paint samples
for imaginary walls.
On weekends and after work
he poured cement, nailed the frame.
I hated the thought of living there.

Hated, too, his blue pickup named for an old girlfriend.
I wonder if he thinks of my mother
or of me, if he owns a new truck with her name.
I can't remember the names of his kids,
a boy and a girl, loud and annoying
he threatened with a belt.

His words build themselves around me.
Never be afraid to throw the first punch.
A man should be able to use his hands.
It's a black-and-blue world.
They become the life we share
and the one we didn't.

On the dirt floor of the someday living room
we looked out to his waterside stake,
a framed door open to brackish air.
He'll never get it done, said my sister.
My brother was three.
He doesn't remember any of this.

He had a shock of red hair, boyish good looks.
He made things with his hands: a copper sculpture for my sister.

Drinking kept him young and talking and sad.
On a dinner menu he drew my mother perfectly in purple crayon.

One night he slept on our lawn.
A man can remake anything about himself except his blood.

Years later, she said, *You know, he was never all there.*
One night he slept on our roof.

Forgive us absence. Forgive us desire.
I wanted him to stay.

I CALL my sister to see what I've forgotten.

The Paddle Wheel, his riverboat restaurant
I dreamed of inheriting.
He owned too a handlebar mustache waxed and twirled
like an Old West sheriff.

I remember unfiltered Camels, his shirts
heavy with pine and Lava soap.
Divorced, widowed, divorced.
Everything he loved was bad luck.

There's a poem below this one
where I know more. A poem
like an unseaworthy vessel
undone and adrift.

A poem with his name. His voice
singing off-key behind the bar.
My mother waiting
all night at the house.

He was a different kind of wisdom poet—
faith in real estate, rolls of Lifesavers,
and Amway. He sold cleaning supplies
and cologne from his Buick's backseat,
slowly building his sales empire:
Jim, Mr. and Mrs. Meyers,
the guy with black hair plugs.

At the sales conventions, men in suits,
Diamond- and Platinum-level sellers,
gold bracelets dazzling as their smiles,
gave rousing speeches: In America,
anything! Forget rags, hello riches.
No one ever said cleaning products.

He said dream a lot. Dream big!
Cadillac, Pebble Beach, white mansion
with a marble foyer, a swimming pool.
He was the loudest guy on the floor,
shook every hand, sang every ballad.

I was a true believer. A disciple.
I read the books on power and influence—
a man's name is the sweetest sound to him.
To learn by heart every person's name
at a party or function, write each one
on a cocktail napkin. Hello Bob,
this must be your wife (napkin) Susan.

I tried a language against my own—his.
Problems were now challenges.
A letdown, an opportunity.
The glass isn't half empty, or half full.
The glass is full, and I will break it
on the kitchen floor if you disagree.

THERE IS no poem below this one—

like an X-ray arriving at bone, ghosted
below pinchable, forgetting skin—

as close as I can go: a moment
when the world begins

again and again. Stopped
at a red light she begins to cry.

Because I am her son I understand
the spark of her sorrow

isn't this day or weather
or song on the radio.

I write this without blame or pity.
This isn't about her, or them.

I study her face and see myself
waiting for the end of waiting.

The light changes and the car
glides towards home.

ENVOI

        —forgive me
mistakes, half-
truths, my own wrong
angles of forgetting.

And remembering.
Names catch my breath
when said aloud, they gift
and curse the present:

we are what happens by accident.
Suitor, from the Latin *secutor*,
to follow. I can't
catch them, or let them go—

LIFEGUARD

My father is modest. He didn't save hundreds
from drowning. Just a few dozen.
Gathered from the swell, the riptide, rough,
rough waves he carried them ashore.

Half-lit, he tells it again. The storm
against sky, the lifeguard without fear
alone in the water, the crowd
gathered to witness.

              Here's what to notice:
the danger of weather, failures
of the other people to help, we never know
what happened to the boy.

This is my humblebrag, my bravado,
my foolish affection
to write the same poem year after year.
In some versions I am the lifeguard.
In others I'm drowning.
Then I'm sky. Then wave.

ARS POETICA

Sometimes I dream of the son
I do not have. My blood only goes backwards.
My ear is threadbare.
My eye is plain.

I don't need a poem to remind me
how difficult it is to remain
just one person. Today the tailor
at the laundromat smiled
as he took my shirt to mend.

Tuesday, he said. *Or Wednesday.* I trust
the back and forth between days
and selves. In love, I'm out of love.
Out of love, it's all I want.

TASHLICH

Since you have no bread in your pockets
                you throw your keys into the water
                        watch them sink,
silvered at the stone bottom in late daylight.

                Since you can't start your car or open the locked
doors of your house, since you can't get back

you strip off your tie and shirt, your socks, shoes, and pants;
                      your shirt's plastic buttons glisten
like fish eyes and zippers gnash their teeth.

                    Bills from your wallet
slip downstream, dark like a promise—
you have more to cast away:

                the watch from your wrist, a name,
shame, a stubborn reflection that holds to you
                    as you hold to it,
your father's voice, your mother's eyes.

New Economy

A man tries to trade his guitar for a city bus.
My pick for your passengers. Six strings for sixteen wheels.

A bride on her wedding day exchanges her love
for bright weather, a groom exchanges his hands for hers.

A father offers to trade his family for a hotel's worth of sleep.
A sailor offers the Pacific for a hotel's worth of sex.

Tonight, the shirt from my back, my singing mouth,
my endless praise for your skin or company.

I'll give you my stethoscope for a red barn: a doctor.
I'll give you my right arm for your left: his patient.

It's the inequality of pain a sleepless woman wants
to give away. Here, take mine, she offers to freight trains

whistling their replies through the city's poorest wards:
Jealousy gets you jealousy. Rage gets you rage.

"What wouldn't you offer?" a man asks the pawnshop window.
"What wouldn't you take?" replies the glass.

JV Wrestling

We struck the mats,
        call and answer:
No Mercy. No Mercy.
           Our songs of command.
Strong arm. Throw legs.
           Crush the lung. This, I learned,
is my body: resistance
        and tenderness
and permission. After practice
        we cleaned our dirt
and blood. Wet towels
        pushed on all fours,
a phalanx of boys,
        stench of my own sweat,
the one next to me
        and the one beside him,
so that home, after showering
        I could still taste
our animal flesh
        as I collapsed into bed
too tired to re-dress.

My Father Buys Land in a Town Called Happy Adventure

The chainsaw is a beautiful animal—
restless hunger and speed, a buck
in the woods: *What I touch is marked,*
entered. By force is the way of my father.
Cut and drag. We clear the stand
of fall. Nothing's said without
gesture. Next winter's heat, stacked
to season. To season, a verb
of entering. Enter salt air, strong wind.
Enter cool evenings, spring light.
Enter patience. Enter time. All day, a joke
eases between us: call this place
My Inheritance. Call this place *Home*
Away from Home. Call it *End of the Line.*
Call it *His Kingdom.* Call it mine.

The Haber Problem

1.

More than a few parallels between my father and Fritz Haber: scientists, Jews, storytellers, obsessive, organized, thoughtful, ambitious, difficult, intelligent, stubborn, exiles, husbands, fathers, sons. I want to add more but there is only so much I know about both men.

My father's biography is in progress. A university website gives little beyond the facts. He is an "internationally recognized" oceanographer who studies "microbial food web dynamics and their influence on the cycling of organic material on ocean-climate interactions." In other words, he studies the water and wants more.

For a moment I am a boy in his laboratory. Maps of water, blue current lines, fill the walls. The lab is a greenhouse of fluorescent light, a solarium of test tubes and beakers, lab coats, radiation symbols—all bright and clean. Lab techs and grad students lean over microscopes, make marks in green notebooks. I can name the parts of the compound light microscopes: arm, stage, light, diaphragm, eyepiece, projector lens and condenser lens. Project and condense. One lens throws forth and the other focuses. In the far corner, his old wood desk: paint-stained reading lamp, stacks of paper, half-filled coffee mugs, old issues of *Limnology and Oceanography, Science,* and *Nature.*

I've been published in all of those, he'd tell you, even if you didn't ask.

Tonight, my father and I are not speaking. We're each waiting for the other to change the subject. We're sitting in his kitchen, and it's snowing outside. He's wearing a blue T-shirt. Pipes in the opened ceiling drip water into a silver pot. A steady rhythm taps against the weather of our argument.

Fucking idiots, he says about whoever bent the copper pipe instead of using an elbow fitting.

The bend is a place of stress. What breaks us from our silence, finally, is the bursting of the pipe. Water streams from the ceiling. He runs to the basement to turn off the main. I stand below and hand tools up to him, as I did when I was young, helping patch the pipe so that we can have water for a few minutes in the morning. A plumber will come tomorrow, he says. We've done all we can do.

He pours two glasses of Jack Daniels and we talk about this hundred-year-old house, its quirks and pleasures. Full glasses, empty glasses. We don't talk about anything we can't see or touch. It's how we are best together, talking around anything that could mean the past is not forgotten.

2.

WHEN I think of Fritz Haber I think of the baby carriage falling down the stairs in the 1925 silent movie *Battleship Potemkin*. I remember too my then-girlfriend, her head against my shoulder, the radiator's heat against the cold Chicago winter as we watched the slow-motion progress of the pram as it tumbled down, step by marble step, saying, "Look at the angle of the camera. Eisenstein was a genius for his time."

1915. France. Haber stands on a small hill and directs the German army to fire the chlorine canisters, the weaponized gas he helped invent. Green smoke rises from the far trenches. Haber, four years at the helm of the Kaiser Wilhelm Institute for Physical Chemistry, is not a military man. He volunteered for service. He wants this to happen. His uniform is handmade. He points to the tanks, orders generals where to fire the 150 tons of chlorine that were released that day, the wind as dangerous as bullets.

The camera studies his face—gold-rimmed glasses, slight frame, bald, manicured mustache—for some detail of explanation. A life defies focus under the lens. "[Haber] considered it his duty," one biographer writes, "and that was the Prussian in him. It was his duty as a scientist to work with all his might for the goals of the state, to win the war."

Or to let Haber explain his purpose during wartime: "A scientist belongs to his country in times of war and to all mankind in times of peace."

How does one write back to a history book and say, No, I disagree?

In the belief of a cause, body counts are statistics added and analyzed. The figures vary, but between 5,000 and 15,000 Allied troops were killed or wounded that day. German troop losses were in the hundreds. And yet, I later read, "Gas warfare, while a psychological weapon, never was a decisive factor in the war."

I recently re-watched *Battleship Potemkin*. I had forgotten that the scene with the baby carriage is also one of massacre. Soldiers dressed all in white march down the stairs firing bullets into the crowd. The carriage released because the child's mother has been shot. I'd forgotten too how many stairs they have to descend, all of them, the men with the guns, and the crowd attempting to flee to safety.

3.

THIS IS a story of before and after. Haber's Nobel year, 1918, came years after his most significant work. The Haber-Bosch process uses high pressure to produce ammonia at an industrial scale. This isn't the glamorous science of relativity or black holes. He didn't question the nature of the soul or explain time and space. This is about the body and hunger. Haber would describe it differently: "[P]ractical usefulness was not the preconceived goal of my experiments." It's about the process for Haber, about what can be known.

Haber's discovery made artificial fertilizers available to the world, from the poorest countries and subsistence farmers to rich nations and agribusiness, transforming how much can be grown and how people eat. Inscribed on the medal they give for the Nobel Prize: *Inventas vitam iuvat excoluisse per artes.* And they who bettered life on earth by new-found mastery.

This isn't false but isn't the whole story.

After France, Haber returned home to Berlin and his wife Clara, his childhood sweetheart and an accomplished chemist herself. Days later she shot herself in her heart. With his Army pistol. Perhaps it was the P08 Parabellum, what we now know as the Luger. Their twelve-year-old son Hermann found her body in the garden. She left no note.

Some saw her suicide as a rebuke to Haber's dedication to chemical warfare. "What Fritz has achieved in these eight years, I have lost—and even more," Clara wrote to a friend. "And what's left fills me with the deepest dissatisfaction."

As a young man, early in his career, Haber said of science, "It is not enough to seek and to know; we must also apply."

This is the problem with Fritz Haber, claims one historian: "People don't know whether to admire him, or despise him. On the one hand, you have the inventor of ammonia synthesis—the benefactor of humanity. On the other, you have the gas warrior, the terrible husband, who drove his wife to commit suicide."

She underestimates our capacity to experience a paradox of feeling in the same moment. There's a story of Gorky and Tolstoy out for a stroll in Moscow. They see a group of soldiers heading in their direction. Tolstoy says, "That's everything that's wrong with our country. Agression, violence, nationalism." Gorky nods attentively. As the soldiers pass them by, they hear the rattle of their sabers and smell their cologne. "That's everything great about our country," Tolstoy says. "Honor, pride, sacrifice." Gorky writes it down.

In 1920, Haber remarried a younger woman who told a biographer he was "a great storyteller."

4.

MY FATHER sometimes tells stories of growing up in Brooklyn in the late 1950s and early 1960s: younger brother, last born, rebellious kid. In one tale, he is a barker on the Coney Island boardwalk, hustling for money from city tourists down for a day at the beach. In another he put himself through grad school by throwing and selling pottery. In all these stories, there are constants, themes that thread and tie: I came up the hard way. I am smarter than most men. I listen with shame and pride when he explains his recent publication or the conference he's attending in France. Is every father, I wonder, a window?

I gather small traces of their lives. Haber's biography on the Nobel Prize website describes him as "Always approachable and courteous, he was interested in every kind of problem. He welcomed administrative responsibilities in addition to research work. A man of forceful personality, he left a lasting impression on the minds of all his associates." I'm happy to find this, and then later a description of him as a "romanticist in courtship, in conversation, and in companionship." I feel for a moment that I'm seeing him beyond the man in the lab coat or military uniform. He's laughing at a joke, helping a colleague solve an equation, dancing with a childhood sweetheart, his hand on the small of her back.

What about the bad days? What about the day he had a cold and fought with his wife over their morning tea? Or the days he mourned his first wife's absence? Only later do I realize when I write about the bad days I'm not writing about one man or the other. They start to overlap, like a tide over the shoreline.

I line up the photos: my grandfather at twenty wearing a black one-piece as he poses beside the white lifeguard stand. Then the photo of my father in his Speedo, teal blue, his muscular body. A woman, not my mother, hangs on his arm. Sunglasses reflect the sky burning above water. Photo of me at sixteen, new lifeguard, as I lean on the pool's metal guard chair.

See how clearly we smile, flex our muscles. We all thought about how that moment would look, weeks, months, years later. We asked ourselves, how would someone see this? How will they judge the curve of my bicep and the definition of my stomach? How will they see this man in the photo—romantic, sturdy, willing to risk his life for another, and of course, handsome? We believe in the body, its shape, tone, and beauty.

5.

OUR LAST family vacation. My sister and I are most impressed we're staying in the same place where they filmed *Dirty Dancing*. The movie takes place in the 1960s at a Borscht Belt resort in the Catskills. We're in late 1980s Virginia. My sister and I spend our days trying to match scenes from the movie with their real locations: dance floor, gazebo, the rock that juts from the lake. In the housekeeping cabin, just up from the water and the sandy beach, my sister and I share one room and my parents share the other. Each night the screen door is left unlatched. We eat in the dining hall with all the other families.

One night, my father is in, as we would all say, a mood. Our food is bad; the service is bad. He calls the waiter incompetent and demands to speak to the manager. This isn't what I've paid for, he says. The manager doesn't know—and we can't say—this isn't about lukewarm chicken à la king, but something else, an anger he carries like a pocket watch.

My father says dinner is inedible. The manager is apologetic but this is, he gestures around, all they have, a set menu. My father is causing a scene. Dinner guests, the other families, here for a nice meal on a clear summer night, a sky full of fireflies and stars, pretend not to notice. They keep eating. Others put down their forks and turn around for a better view. My mother wants to stay. He wants to go. Now they are arguing. And then he goes. He leaves us sitting there, like the wake behind a boat. We finish our dinner. They separate later that year.

Then it's a new century. Fifteen years later. We live four time zones away but tonight we're together, my father and I. It's after midnight. We're on the futon couch in the upstairs room of his house. We're watching TV, and he's beginning to fall asleep. His head falls forward then jerks back, like a quick jab pushing up the chin.

You awake? I ask. Just resting my eyes, he says.

We laugh. He puts his hand on the back of my head. It rests there, and we watch a movie we have both seen before. A gesture that means everything we do not say. Outside, snow dusts the electric wires and tree branches. Yellow lights flash against the window as a salt truck passes below.

I'm tired of silence, that anvil of it, but I don't say anything, my father's son in this moment and in all the ones that follow. I put my arm over his shoulder. He starts to fall asleep, head nodding forward and then back, forward then back.

A friend wrote, "Scratch consumption and you'll find rage, scratch rage and you'll find sadness." But what's below sadness? What's below that? I'm trying to see a life vertically, as far down as I can go. But there's a place where imagination or guessing takes over, and I'm no longer looking at Haber or my father, but myself.

Yes, every father is a window. And in the right light, that window can be a mirror.

6.

It's RAINING. The train is crowded and hot. A woman with too many bags argues with a porter on the platform. Haber leans his head against the glass and takes off his glasses, holds them in one hand. With the thumb and forefinger of his other hand he rubs his eyes. Haber, who wanted nothing more than to help his country, is forced to leave Germany. Even though he converted to Christianity, he's unwelcome after Hitler's rise to power. He will never return.

Perhaps he remembered his days aboard the ocean liner *Hansa* collecting ocean water in order to extract its invisible gold. In every body of water there are minerals broken down and measured in parts per million. His calculations suggested he could gather enough wealth for Germany to repay its war debt. The overlap between Haber the scientist and Haber the nationalist continued after the war. His calculations were wrong.

This is not a tragedy. Not Faust before the fire or Midas with his greed. Those are different myths of before and after. This is a romance. A love story between a man and his faith in himself, between a man and the world he trusted, between a man and his fate. Albert Einstein wrote about Haber, "At the end, he was forced to experience all the bitterness of being abandoned by the people of his circle, a circle that mattered very much to him, even though he recognized its dubious acts of violence . . . It was the tragedy of the German Jew: the tragedy of unrequited love."

Water on the train windows, a border crossing, a new country, and I'm trying to imagine if he knew then he would never go back. It's the same kind of imagination I used to picture my father aboard his polar research cruises. Ice and ice and ocean. Five months gone. Three months gone. When my brother was born, my father was gone. I know him best by departures and arrivals.

I remember standing on the dock and watching his boat return, an admixture of relief and worry. The concrete pillions and the mangy scavenger birds with plastic in their bills, the cornflower sky, the salt air, our nervous anticipation. They get off the boat, one by one. I recognize him at a distance. His beard is longer, but he looks the same. We all embrace.

He stays at the dock to help organize the unloading of the samples. We drive home without him.

When my father returned, the house had to readjust to his presence. I don't mean us, his children, or my mother, but the physical house had to learn again how quick and heavy his footsteps were on the stairs leading up to his study. The house tensed under his shape.

For months at a time we weren't father and son. Instead we were the voices of those things, shades without form, ideas of each other, speaking every couple weeks over the HF radio lines, the connection between McMurdo Station and the outside world. How are you? Over. Fine. Over.

7.

JORGE LUIS BORGES's short story "The Gospel According to Mark" claims there are two human narratives. In the first a man sails the Mediterranean in search of his lost island. In the second a god becomes a man and lets himself be crucified on Golgotha. My father's story is more the first than the second. What was my father's beloved isle? Was it my mother? Or was it the body of the woman he was seeing on the side? Was it the town where we lived? Our house with the wrap-around porch? My sister? Me? Home, away, home.

My father didn't run out in the middle of the night. He didn't leave my mother and me stranded at a highway truck stop. He didn't abandon us like my mother's grandfather, who, in perhaps apocryphal family lore, left his wife and children in the Bronx during the Depression. He vanished. His name was never said aloud.

My father didn't disappear. Or die. No, this is both easier to understand and more complicated. At age fourteen, full of righteous indignation, I confronted him in the hallway of his new house. I asked him why. Why absence? Why did he leave for all those stretches of time? I didn't say it like that. There was more rage. There was more accusation for a hurt I couldn't fully explain but felt.

This, he said, is how I make a living. He didn't say it like that. There was more pain in his voice. I slammed my door. The conversation ended. He loves the work and needs it too. It defines who he is and how he sees himself in the world. This, I think, is his beloved isle. Perhaps, mine too. He sails around the world, from here to elsewhere, never quite satisfied, though always, he likes to believe, in command of his own destiny. His favorite poem is "Invictus." "I am the master of my fate, / I am the captain of my soul."

8.

THE MORE I read about Haber, the more he becomes like a character in a novel, fictional and intimate. When I say *Fritz* I am his wife. When I say *Vater* I am his son. *Herr Haber*, and I'm his colleague at the Institute. I fear that if Haber turns into a character, my father becomes a character. I become a character. A cliché theme I can't escape—absent father, lost son—and the story is no longer my own.

But this isn't a book I'm reading under the covers late at night. There is no scene where he kneels down, squares his shoulders to mine and says, "Take care of your mother. You're the man of the house now." He didn't say it when he left for the Antarctic, or when they split, not the first or second time or the one that was final.

The truth is this: We didn't miss him when he was gone. Not entirely. Life found a rhythm and a pace. It didn't seem strange, but expected. Winter on the East Coast meant summer in another hemisphere, the season when planes landed without too much trouble and the daily, difficult work of research continued. We continued too.

Fritz Haber had a son in his second marriage, and this son became a history professor who wrote a book about chemical warfare in World War I. "Thus fear and uncertainty continue," Ludwig Fritz Haber writes. "Do we have to live with them? I am sure we have to, but I also think that, as time passes, we will learn to live with our anxieties."

I search the book's index for the word father. Or son. Neither word is there.

"Where does the truth lie?" the son writes in *The Poisonous Cloud*. "This is dangerous ground for an historian. But it is worth exploring . . . in order to give a rounded picture of the effect of this extraordinary weapon."

When not a scientist, my father is a revisionist historian. He'd accuse me of the same thing. We each have a different memory of what kind of man he was in those years. He'd probably describe himself as dependable, generous, caring. All of these adjectives would be accurate depictions of him.

Where does the truth lie? "A story cannot be entirely true and good at the same time," Haber is claimed to have said.

Before becoming a scientist, Haber, awkward and unsure, briefly and unsuccessfully worked for his father's export business. To explain how an unconfident man found his voice, one biographer relates this fantastical account:

> One very warm summer day he went hiking in the Swiss mountains. After a jaunt of eight hours, searching for drinking water, he came to a very small, seemingly uninhabited place. Water was not to be found, and he was very thirsty. Finally, he saw a well surrounded by a low wall. He immediately immersed his entire head. At almost the same time and unnoticed by him, a bull had done likewise; neither paid much attention to the other. But when they withdrew from the water, they found their heads had been interchanged. Fritz Haber had a bull's head and prospered as a professor that eventful day.

One might read Haber's mystical transformation as a metaphor for his drive or potency. But it is also the story of a man becoming a monster. In the Greek myth, the Minotaur, terrible offspring of Pasiphaë and the Cretan bull, is King Minos's punishment by the gods for greed and disobedience. This lesson reoccurs again and again in myths: there is a price to be paid for challenging the gods.

In 1934, exiled, on his way to Palestine, Haber died. A heart attack. Alone in a hotel room in Basel, Switzerland. He didn't witness the deaths, on scales both large and small: his son Hermann, or the millions, relatives and strangers, that would die in concentration camps. This dark inheritance: the early formulations of Zyklon B were developed in his laboratory.

I want to show Haber this, and say look. This is what you've done. Explain the wrong. Explain the good.

9.

IN AN ESSAY published in the July 1947 issue of *American Scientist*, Morris Goran of Roosevelt College in Chicago offered an apologia for Haber. He writes, "Unfortunately he is remembered most often for introducing poison gas on a large scale during World War I. But in this he can no more be indicted than can Leonardo da Vinci, the atomic scientists, or the recent soldiers of the laboratory who develop synthetics and substitutes. Science has become a functional activity, being controlled by whatever forces control society."

Goran, the author of *Experimental Biology for Boys* and *Experimental Chemistry for Boys*, and the father of three girls, went on to write *The Story of Fritz Haber* in 1967. The book ends with a quote from the Nobel Prize citation praising Haber's "service of his country and all mankind."

Daniel Charles's book about Haber, *Master Mind*, ends with a return to the question of the value of science and technology to solve the world's problems. "Sometimes," Charles writes, "it's the duty of an honest scientist to dash all hope that technology will rescue humanity from its folly. Sometimes, science can not save us."

The Alchemy of Air, a book on Haber and Carl Bosch, concludes with the sentence, "Hermann Haber, Fritz and Clara's son, committed suicide after the war." An image of death following death, loss following loss: direct, razor-like, indicting.

The events don't change. They unfold exactly as they always have. What changes is our sightline. "Let us be gentle when we question our fathers," writes one poet. I remember the day when I saw in my father the body of my grandfather. As if an explanation of how little our anger matters.

10.

WE'RE NOT so different, my father likes to say. I write research proposals and scientific papers, and you write what you write.

He's right. And wrong. We share more than the fact we both put marks on paper. We want to get to a place below the surface. To know what can't be seen at first, and hold it up for others to see.

At the end of his Nobel speech, a speech that is technically astute, deferential to colleagues who proceeded him, and otherwise uninspiring in its prose, Haber says, "improved nitrogen fertilization of the soil brings new nutritive riches to mankind and that the chemical industry comes to the aid of the farmer who, in the good earth, changes stones into bread." The last lines are beautiful and strange and enchanting.

The farmer is an alchemist who in "good earth" changes "stones" into "bread." This is Haber. And my father. This is where the artist and scientist find their common vocabulary—a desire for transformation. A desire for a new story.

I'm thinking again about my body, its mortal limits. And then I'm thinking about his. At the same moment I'm imagining the unnameable loss I'll feel at his death, I feel something like lightness. The expectations of who I am, or who I should become, the reminder of the personality traits we share and I can't, for all my trying, shake, the witness to who I was and who I have become, will all be gone. I feel the world opening, a mercy, and I wonder how I will live in that world. I'm ashamed by this thought.

The summer I spent in Turkey I came down with a terrible flu. I lost hearing in one ear. He was the first person I called. He is the first person I call for advice about running, health, and cooking. I don't call him for advice about relationships. When he dies who will I call when I have a fever? Who will I call when I need advice about jobs? Or home repair? Or money? Who will I ask about what kind of roasting pan to buy? A day when I'll have a number and name in my phone for someone I can never call.

TWO

The Suitors

To THE men and women whose names I've erased
a warning I offer too late.

Never trust a man who asks to be tied
down to the bed with strong rope

but then adds, *not too tight.*
Never trust a man who is good with words.

I FELL in love with the most unremarkable man I knew.

Soundman for theater productions and something
of a know-it-all about wiring house lights to cue
blustery entrances and exits.
He was not that kind of guy.

I'd watch him work, imagine taking off
his heavy black glasses, heat
of our breath on winterized windows.

I dreamed his body in his absence.
Longing arcs towards action.
But not yet. Not him.

It was a one-sided affair
unrequited as weather.

SHE FELL first for my arms.
Pretty is not a word she'd use
under normal circumstances
but exceptions can be made

for two salmon swimming upstream,
two aspens strong against
the winter wind, twin
ridgelines of promise.

I fell for her hips. Inlets
of her shoulders, range
of her spine. I fell
for myself in her eyes.

She took my virginity
in the bed of my younger brother.
Out of pity. Or kindness.
Or wonder to touch
and be touched.

When I'm older, she said,
I'll only love men
who know to go down on me
without me asking.

She wanted a man
who could offer his affections
like loaves or fishes.
She wanted—as I wanted—
to be older, or wiser,

another lover, another life.
Fall, we say, as if the body
slips to ground, unhurt.
And then, we get up.

In the dark we gathered
our clothes—said nothing—
just the sound of buttons
snapped, shirts pulled,
our backs to each other.

AND THERE I was, *doing cocaine*
off a guy's ass, he told me. Name-dropper,
big-shot producer, nice teeth, and jeans
with a blazer. I didn't get the joke.
He was an out-of-towner. I was nobody.
The seduction wasn't hard.

I wrote this poem years ago
but left out the facts.
I am a different kind of lover
of truth now. The scene is the same.
White branches, white sidewalks.
Always snowing. We were high
in his hotel room. The TV, on.
The window, ajar. The air, cold.

He put his hand through my hair.
I closed my eyes. All I had to do
was stay. In the end, nothing happened:
problematic, unsatisfying end.
Or maybe that's all I wanted.

To go home alone. To write a poem
where he becomes you, and I become a figure
borrowed from a book, a shepherd in Sicilian pastures
singing with the pleasure of knowing
no reply would come:

I am a man in empty fields
with only pious clouds and dumb animals
for company. With only words
for lovers.

HER MOTHER warned her to never date a writer.
Or become one.
They have no skills in this world
just lies and sweet talk
mixing up the story they tell
and the story they live.

She found a new mother
honest as flint who wrote
I'm a lucky bitch. A toast
to make to afternoon bartenders
and empty icehouses where she drank
alone and without regret.

Reckless with her money and talents,
she cheated, more than once.
Said it to my face.
Said too I was good in bed.
She meant it. But it doesn't mean

I miss her voice whispering,
It's the space below your hips,
or she misses the messages I left
when I knew she wasn't home.

HE WAS no conversationalist.
I said it to his face. He shrugged. *Who cares?*

It was the truth. I was in it for his youth.
His body, long and fit like a gazelle, handsome
as hell, a drug against thinking
too much about anything but pleasure.

When I think of him now, I think of Diane Arbus,
her photographs of strangers embracing
in parks, undressing in bathrooms,
or alone at a neon dive.

This is about flesh, I said, my dumb
pride to want nothing beyond his body.
Not his certainty, but his hands.
Not his pity, but his teeth.

Arbus, who trusted the honest accounting
of skin, said of her images:
*They are proof that something was there
and no longer is. Like a stain.*

*And the stillness of them is boggling.
You can turn away but when you come back
they'll still be there looking at you.*

GOD, HE was beautiful.

His reckless, easy way,
eyes bright as pearl snap-buttons
forked lightning smile and

not to brag he was famous
in some circles.

St. Augustine: *Make me chaste Lord—*
but not yet.

His parents were cattle farmers in Wyoming.
He wore shit-kickers, animal skin boots

brown as a common thrush, white top stitching:
attention-getter, ornate song,

calling, *my foot fits on your neck,*
calling, *foolish boy, easy mark.*

The love poem risks
abandonment, of speaking too soon.
Or too late.

The next morning we slept. White sheets
like full sails.

This is no love poem.

SHE LOVED Cindy Sherman. Those photos. Those hands
how they angle
to unfurl, slide under a knee

              or reach out
      like a mind's blink of recognition.
Unsettled and unsettling.

           Some people think she's uncanny.
I did, embarrassed.
She sang on the subway. She was clumsy with scissors.

     Once, she nicknamed our waitress Tits
     and told her.
Call it ardor!
Call it license!

      She thought I wanted to change her,
      make her soft as Lamb's Ear,
      a breezy-eyed girl, giggle and sigh.

Or the dutiful wife—
matching socks, roasting roasts
tsk-tsking my bad habits.

        But what I liked best—
when she was coy and hard to get.

Photo still. An image
I recognize and can't touch.

On the television of Boysroom,
a bar name too clever by half,
two men fuck a third in a jungle. It's a theme.
Combat boots and camouflage shorts
fallen to their ankles.
They're trying to act at ease.

Sometimes all I want is refusal,
to be told no, not you.
But tonight, I want to go home
with a handsome stranger whose name
I forget as soon as it is said.

When I describe his tongue
in my mouth, his hand down my back,
what I mean is I'm disappointed.
He takes off his clothes too quickly.
I want the slow undoing.
There's no mystery to his body
and that's all there is.

Months later, in another city,
I think of the elevator key he needed
to start the lift to the roof,
steel bridges and glass windows,
a whole city of possibility.

To look under the clothes of a man
for answers, to touch his skin
and think flesh is meaning—
I record this error too.
I take notes. I make revisions.

This time, daylight.
Light, our measure.
I refuse to praise the dark.
I name every name.

ENVOI

The single spiral of an orange peel
wound over the core of an apple—
imperfect as the marriage
of memory and desire.
Our bodies hunger
and can't remember for what.

I drove by your house, crush
of leaves under wheel,
just to know you once lived there.
You keep asking to be held
close or forgotten.
I want both.

THE YEAR

I broke every window.
The year I stole every library book.
The year I lived below the El,
always the hum, running through and by
of people who desired to be arrived.
I couldn't see them but knew wanting.
The year I didn't sleep.
None of this tells how on the tri-corner of 23rd,
Broadway, and Fifth I called into the gusts
my fault my fault.
None of this says sorrow. And means it.
Trains run through me. I am not a train.
Air touches my skin. I am not sky.
I don't need to believe each time I curse
God, or go home with a stranger,
or refuse decision
the spaces in my body widen, are deep like a well,
bone dry, and halfway to China.
I've done nothing wrong. I've done it all.
Redemption, take my name.
Ask me inside. Let me enter.
A house inside a house.
A prayer inside a prayer.

The Next Row

              I used to think after rain lashed the fields
behind my house and listed its complaints
against the window

                        like a post office clerk
tapping at the nothing there and the anything

that might cross his counter, it would be clear again.
I could see every edge of every blade
                         cut the sky in two.

The woman in the next row
          shares your skeptical brow and razor

cut hair; shares your ability to look at ease and unhappy at once.
        Is she proof of you the way an umbrella is proof of rain?

Plush red seats and jumbo plastic holders, a couple wrapped
arm to arm; we are this

            and more inside our silver house, our eyes
grown generous as puddles, and further within, a psalm:
I know you I know you.

               Do you remember, I want to ask,
it was winter before we went downtown, you stood
at the mirror (the apartment's panes gleaning ice) and drew
dark lines above your eye?
                Eye to hand to eye.

I know you: I'm getting it wrong. *I know you*: her face, the blade
        of a cattail raising its furrowed head,

           the projector's white eye, light cast forward,
                divided inside this wide wide frame.

Amanda Lepore

I love you dear lips like overripe watermelons blossoming
their crimson bellies. I love when you wear windows
of black and lace. I love you like golden trophies
or collections of '70s porn under the mattresses
of all my boyhood homes. I love you like a quickie
in the dressing room of Macy's, or small, golden
whispers between girlfriends in verdant city parks.
Or your bombshell coif—all shellac and gloss.
Or your narrow waist, like the northern edge
of the Flatiron. I love you and your sea otter sway.
I love not knowing where you go in daytime,
who zips you out of your dress, who writes
their name on your back's kitten skin, their fingers
opening the mouth of every vowel as they write
you fan letters, hymns, summons, and requests.
I love you tonight in the glamour of our unrequited
affections, in catcalls and applause, in the wide
spotlight, those colored gels which hide us, give us
away, make every face ripen like cold, green fruit.

Suitor's Dream

I say you and mean our life together
will be a picturesque postcard

from the Cape of Good Cheer,
the Cape of Wonder.

Other days it will be a typhoon,
warm waters gathered into storm.

I am divided
and unsure in so many things

except this:
the end of every suitor is rest.

To touch the hem of your dress
or the seam of your suit

and leave it. The body waits.
We have the serious business

of living: unpack boxes
of books, unroll newspaper

from glasses, fill cabinets
with bowls and measuring cups.

We invite our friends.
Join us. We've made a place at our table,

the table we bought at the flea market
and carried five blocks home.

I set it with your plates
and my silverware.

He Closes His Eyes in Pleasure, or the Description of It

Another man undresses him.
He looks too young.

His balls are shaved, his cock
thick as a Coke bottle.

He closes his eyes in pleasure,
or the description of it.

Then, open, he looks off-screen
for a cue—the moment he has a sister

in North Forks and a mother
in the ground. An uncle

blind as a lizard, a friend
who owes him fifty bucks.

He's supposed to be in character—
cowboy, student, patient—

just walked into a room
of waiting sex, though

we're far enough in I've forgotten
which he is, or was.

I close my eyes over his,
not the ones finishing

in ecstasy, but slightly bored,
rent to pay, train to catch,

wondering where next
he'll put his open mouth.

The Ad

The ad I answered asked for me
    or the man I wanted
to be. On paper we sing.
    In flesh we're off-key.
We gossiped over tabouli:
    local celebrities who dined
here alone and the famous artist's
    museum show,
words scrolled
    in storms of red light.
We never got to the rough
    stuff he promised, a test
of strength to know
    who could take the other
in a fight of play
    that is not play.
The rest is a body stripped,
    stronger than it looks.
I didn't think this would happen
    like this, he said.
I didn't either, I lied.
    I know too well
the coming end.
    He called for a week
without answer
    then stopped.
The man I promised
    to be—taller, surer,
content—left too.
    On paper I sing.
In flesh I run.

Suitor's Dream

I want to begin again.

      Your buckle undone, an eye
opened, the snap clicked
one half from the other—

          It's the moment before
skin, before clothes pattern the floor
like samba steps, this neck
with hand, this waist
with this mouth.

We are only the possibility
of an end; I haven't made a promise
I will not keep.

      I want to begin again.
A new desire is an old one rising.
Old mistake. Old news.

      And then it's winter.
Wind lifts snow from ground.
Boughs shimmer trinkets of ice.
These are not for us.

Water for tea boils and wind strikes
our windows, a storm
on every part of the glass.

The kettle raises its mouth of air. Singing
here, you will never be satisfied
with what you have.

Singing, you will break every promise.
      Of course you will.
      Of course you will.

The Docent

Of art deco hotels
he was a kind of expert—who died there,
who slept there—a sly grin, a knowing wink.
Easy charm and wit, ladies with blue hair
loved him like a son. On tours of historic
buildings downtown he knew every architect
but couldn't name what he wanted.
Words escaped me too.

We lied about our first meeting.
We lied to our friends. To each other.
One night he put his hand on my cheek
told me not to worry.
My skin is the wind, his hand a weathervane.
I can't remember why I was upset.
I can't remember what he said, what solace
he named, what shame he didn't.

He walks backwards in my dreams.
He never looks down. His hands offer
this house or that. I walk towards him.
A tour of my old neighborhood:
this garden planted by an oil baron,
this church rebuilt twice. My coy guide,
where are we going? When will we arrive?
What will we call that place?

At Night You Read to Me

Once, you read the essay where the past
    is compared to a lighthouse

as if we climb a metal staircase
    each year and can look

down on our lives, the wild motion
    of days ordered into meaning.

Years later, inside that spine
    of lightness, hours unwound

into angles of remembering,
    I can see the water glass

beside the book on the nightstand,
    a page you folded at its corner—

little lighthouse, little sea—
    our happiness together.

Except, I've got it wrong.
    You never read me the essay

about the lighthouse. It was about a man
    who speaks too late to his father.

Remembers crushing ice
    with the heavy spiral of a rolling pin.

Feeding him broken chips.
    The cool. The hand. The mouth.

If I write again about my father
    may my hands fall off,

my tongue harden to obsidian.
    Or, give me the punishment of myths:

my son will never speak to me,
    or he'll speak to me in that tone, write

every mistake, tell all I've done wrong
    and regret every word.

The End

The end of every suitor is rest.
Joy too. And sorrow. The end
is praise. A wife. A husband.

A joke about a man who loved
the moon. The end is disappointment.
Stand-ins, stopgaps, a waiting

for the right true love to arrive.
A suitor's end is confession
and apology. Silence.

A son with your eyes.
A daughter with your smile.
The end of every suitor

is a myth: of fathers, of lovers,
the dream of a new coast,
a postcard: *Wish you were here.*

Coda

FOR YOU, I'll explain
    the dream:

lemons turning away
    from green—

bright cargo and
    heavy; they fall,

they unhinge,
    they sail like

a hundred swift ships
    sack and burn

then say goodbye.
    For you, I'm through

with need—last, enough,
    no more. Except

we're never without
    that song.

A clique of flies
    core to center.

Sweetness as sweetness
    does in our body

hides under sharp
    white ribs.

A singing of tongues,
    so many I lose count.

I COUNT; I remember
a singing

of tongues.
Their hum. Flies

circling a mason jar.
Paper hive heat.

Voiceless breath—
open, cover, confess;

this wanting and
the mouth it carries

across flesh. Little ship
of hunger.

I'm rapt as a child
hiding in leaves,

reading reds and yellows,
new roof and walls,

luxuries of a home
made of storms,

of rivers, of droughts.
He pretends

to be swallowed.
He is.

We're not
    inside a whale

or cormorant.
    We don't live

in tin drums
    of any belly, hull

or hell, where it's hard
    to tell dark

from dark.
    The problem is light—

a new kind of blind—
    my hands

turn touch to sight
    and like waking see

shape before color
    luck before fate.

And the mind, heartbeat
    slow, awake,

turns a day into
    might.

You might
    with touch

fill the sailcloth
    of my neck,

keel to nest and
    launch to sea,

to island, to palm,
    to sand bleached

as bone, this body
    of possibility:

our life away
    from life.

Think shipwreck.
    Think crash

and shore, deck timbers
    we gather

to burn, and, without
    rescue, live.

LET'S LIVE
        upstate, spell

ourselves in ice.
        In a quiet village

aproned owners salt
        paths to their door.

Pines send snow below.
        White breath,

white room.
        If I think of sea,

tremolo and trade
        the sunstroke waves

light as lemons,
        I'll say nothing.

I'm anchor
        and joy.

I FEAR no anchor
       inked to arm

or neck when I
       undress, no

double barbs of stay
       and stay, flesh

never transparent
       as a house

without walls.
       Each body lives

a hundred lives
       and is silent

about where
       it sleeps.

WE SLEEP.
    We live.

We go back
    to the root

of desire—
    from the stars—

as if we could lash
    light to skin,

and bear it.
    For you

this dream.

Acknowledgments

Thank you to the editors and readers of the following publications in which versions of these poems first appeared:

Memorious: "Coda"; *New Yorker*: "Lifeguard"; *Post Road*: "The Year"; *Quarterly West*: "Suitor's Dream (1)"; *Slate*: "New Economy"; *Salamander*: "*Tashlich*"; *Southern Review*: "The Suitors (1)"; *The Rumpus*: "Amanda Lepore"; *Virginia Quarterly Review*: "The Next Row"; "Suitor's Dream (2)" (as "*Kol Nidre*") received the Anna Davidson Rosenberg Award for Poems on the Jewish Experience.

This book was made possible with generous support from the Fine Arts Work Center in Provincetown, the Sustainable Arts Foundation, the University of Houston Creative Writing Program, the Inprint Brown Foundation, Inprint Houston and the Barthelme Prize, the Dorothy Sargent Rosenberg Memorial Fund, the Stanford University Wallace Stegner fellowship program, the Bread Loaf Writers' Conference, and the University of Southern California Creative Writing and Literature Program.

To Kate Gale, Tobi Harper, Natasha McClellan and everyone at Red Hen, my endless gratitude. Thank you Rob McQuilkin for your sharp vision and belief in my work. For their mentorship and care, I'm grateful to all of my friends and teachers.

I'd especially like to thank the following for their friendship, love, and support: Erin Beeghly, Esme Rivkin, Jacob Rivkin, Jessica Piazza, Darin Ciccotelli, Gerald Maa, Brandon Som, Alen Hamza, Lacy Johnson, Giuseppe Taurino, Paola Tello, Marc McKee, Harriet Clark, Chanda Feldman, Elizabeth Bradfield, Chris Santiago, Mike Scalise, John Evans, Holly Masturzo, Rachel Applegate, Matthew Nienow, Laura McKee, Lisa Iglesias, Paul Gerlitz, Tarfia Faizullah, Rebecca Lindenberg, Casey Fleming, Janalynn Bliss, Alexandra Primiani, Diana Khoi Nguyen, Major Jackson, Gabrielle Calvocoressi, Tom Sleigh, Claudia Rankine, Eavan Boland, W.S. DiPiero, Ken Fields, Peter Balakian, Tony Hoagland, J. Kastley, Marie Ponsot, and David St. John. And most of all, thank you to my family.

Biographical Note

Joshua Rivkin is the author of *Chalk: The Art and Erasure of Cy Twombly*, a New York Times Book Review Editors' Choice and finalist for the 2019 PEN/Jacqueline Bograd Weld Award for Biography. His poems and essays have appeared in the *New Yorker, Slate, Southern Review, Virginia Quarterly Review*, and *Best New Poets*. A former Fulbright Fellow in Rome, Italy, as well as a Stegner Fellow in poetry, he has received awards and scholarships from the Sustainable Arts Foundation, Fine Arts Work Center in Provincetown, and the Bread Loaf Writers' Conference.